As the Sky Begins to Change

As the Sky Begins to Change

poems

Kim Stafford

 Red Hen Press | *Pasadena, CA*

Book design by Mark E. Cull

Library of Congress Cataloging-in-Publication Data

Names: Stafford, Kim Robert, author.
Title: As the sky begins to change: poems / Kim Stafford.
Description: Pasadena, CA: Red Hen Press, 2024.
Identifiers: LCCN 2023038532 | ISBN 9781636281476 (paperback) | ISBN
   9781636281513 (ebook)
Subjects: LCGFT: Poetry.
Classification: LCC PS3569.T23 A88 2024 | DDC 811/.54—dc23/eng/20231002
LC record available at https://lccn.loc.gov/2023038532

The National Endowment for the Arts, the Los Angeles County Arts Commission, the Ahmanson Foundation, the Dwight Stuart Youth Fund, the Max Factor Family Foundation, the Pasadena Tournament of Roses Foundation, the Pasadena Arts & Culture Commission and the City of Pasadena Cultural Affairs Division, the City of Los Angeles Department of Cultural Affairs, the Audrey & Sydney Irmas Charitable Foundation, the Meta & George Rosenberg Foundation, the Albert and Elaine Borchard Foundation, the Adams Family Foundation, Amazon Literary Partnership, the Sam Francis Foundation, and the Mara W. Breech Foundation partially support Red Hen Press.

First Edition
Published by Red Hen Press
www.redhen.org

Acknowledgments and notes on some poems

Cirque: "The Big Empty"; *Limberlost Review*: "Back Then, His Words Were Not Enough"; *Northwest Review*: "Inventory of Light"; *Rattle*: "Calling Home," "The Hard Part"; *Terrain.org*: "Birding for the Blind," "Light in Earth," "Out Oak Island Road"; *Vox Populi*: "The Moth Vote," "Poems for a Cause," "Rainy Day in the 40s," "So Still," "What's Not in the News," "Words of Sugar, Words of Salt"; *Windfall*: "Gone to the Garden."

The Art of Revising Poetry: 21 U.S. Poets on their Drafts, Craft, and Process, ed. Charles Finn and Kim Stafford (London: Bloomsbury, 2023): "Lost in Snow"; *Dear Vaccine: Global Voices Speak to the Pandemic*, ed. David Hassler, Tyler Meier, and Naomi Shihab Nye (Kent OH: Kent State University Press, 2022): "Second Shot"; *I Hope You Find What You're Looking For*, a book of photographs by Gloria Feinstein (Verona, 2022): "Resilience"; *The Madrona Project: The Universe is a Forest*, ed. Michael Daley and Finn Wilcox (Chimacum, WA: Empty Bowl, 2023): "Wood Too Good to Cut"; *The Path to Kindness: Poems of Connection and Joy*, ed. James Crews (North Adams, MA: Storey Publishing, 2022): "A Chair by the Creek."

"After Fire, Rain" owes much to W.S. Merwin's "June Rain."
"Birding for the Blind," "After Fire, Rain," "Out Oak Island Road," and "Why the Beach" were paired with piano selections performed by Hunter Noack for the All Classical Portland FM's "Improvisation Sessions" for broadcast in April 2023.
"The Cardinal Debates the Jay" was written after a presidential debate in the 2019 election cycle and echoes the twelfth-century Middle English poem "The Owl and the Nightingale."
"For the Bird Singing before Dawn" appeared online at Poem-a-Day, from the Academy of American Poets, on April 27, 2022, and later in *Stone Gathering, Too*.
"Furry Dice" recalls when my late friend Douglas Byers invited me to a Hobie Cat sailing race off Port Townsend, Washington, where at peak speed, we flipped the boat and pitch-poled into the drink. I owe him verve.
"In the Children We Will Make Our Home" was composed for a ceremony at the Oregon State Capitol building, when seventeen immigrants became US citizens.
The form of "Lend a Hand" echoes "Samurai Song" by Robert Pinsky.
The second stanza of "Leningrad, 2022" quotes Hitler's personal command for treatment of Russian civilians under siege in the Battle of Leningrad, September 1941 to January 1944, in the Russian city now known as Saint Petersburg. See *Leningrad: Tragedy of a City Under Siege, 1941-44*, by Anna Reid (London: Bloomsbury, 2011), 134-135.
"Lightning, Thunder, Rain" was set to music as a choral work by Marjorie Halloran.
"Moss Offers," "Why I Became an Earth Dweller," "Why No Longer a Wild Bird,"

and "Why the Beach" appeared in *Rain Magazine*. The syntax of "Moss Offers" follows that in "The Hummingbird: a Seduction," by Pattiann Rogers.

"Mother Russia, Wounded by the Modern Tsar" first appeared in *And Blue Will Rise Over Yellow: An International Poetry Anthology for Ukraine*, ed. John Bradley (Kallisto Gaia Press, 2022). Zima Junction is the birthplace of the Russian poet Yevgeny Yevtushenko, whose poem "Babi Yar" recalls the massacre of Ukrainian Jews in World War II. He told me this poem made him welcome in every synagogue in the world.

"Old Codger's Garden of Verses" was written after visiting the home of Robert Louis Stevenson's grandfather in Colinton, Scotland.

"Rich Land Between" was written for an exhibition of paintings by Ellen Goldschmidt.

"The Supremes" was written on the day news came that the US Supreme Court had overturned *Roe v. Wade*.

"Sweeping Dew from Sage" appeared as "Learning Oregon Desert Autobiography" in *High Desert Journal*.

Some of these poems were posted on Instagram (@kimstaffordpoetry) and later reprinted in a series of limited-edition chapbooks from Little Infinities Press:

"After Fire, Rain," "The Cardinal Debates the Jay," "D.C. Weather Report," "The Fauci-Trump Scale of Human Character," "Nurse's Note," "Raccoon in Plum Time," "Schooling Sorrow," "Stranger in the House," "Under My Breath," and "Woman Pumping Gas" appeared in *Seeing 2020* (2021);

"Beyond This War," "Blue," "Calling Home," "Chain of Command," "Chaos Theory," "The Hard Part," "Leningrad, 2022," "Mother Russia, Wounded by the Modern Tsar," "Plum Trees in War," and "Walking on the Dead" appeared in *Sunflower Seeds: Poems for Ukraine* (2022);

"Horses of Iceland" and "Poetry Monger" appeared in *Glacier Blue: Poems in Iceland* (2022);

"Book Store," "Canary in the Mind," "The Monkish Behavior of Trees," "Museum on Fire," "Night Flight of the Screaming Child," "Old Codger's Garden of Verses," and "To Lend a Hand" appeared in *Oddments of the Sacred: Poems in England & Scotland* (2022).

Thanks to the editors and stellar crew at Red Hen Press for welcoming this third book.

Thanks to the Fishtrap summer gathering, and to the artist retreat PLAYA at Summer Lake, where some of these poems were written.

As the Sky Begins to Change is available as an audiobook, read by the author, thanks to Billy Oskay and Klaus Heyne at Big Red Studio.

And thanks to my wife Perrin for her belief in my creative life.

CONTENTS

I.

Earth Verse

2.

Plum Trees in War

3.

Manhood Lost and Found

4.

Your Emily Dickinson Hour

As the Sky Begins to Change

1.

Earth Verse

For the Bird
Singing before Dawn

Some people presume to be hopeful
with no evidence for hope, to be
happy when there is no cause.
Let me say now, I'm with them.

In deep darkness on a cold twig
in a dangerous world, one first
little fluff utters a peep, a warble,
a song—and in a little while, behold:

first glimmer shows, then a glow
filters through misty trees,
then the bold sun rises, then
everyone starts bustling about.

And that first crazy optimist, can we
forgive her for thinking, dawn by dawn,
"Hey, I made that happen!
And oh, life is so fine."

Resilience

Is resilience being strong
as iron, or perennial as grass?
Is resilience standing fast
in storms, or seeking to understand
how old trees, deep-rooted, bend?
Resilient is the one who whispers
at darkest hours, *This, too, shall pass.*
Resilience begins in knowing sorrow,
and ends in finding how to tell its tale.
Resilience mutters in trouble, *I wonder
what we'll learn.* To be resilient, juggle
strength with tenderness, in compassion
stern. Resilience lives through struggle
by thinking beyond struggle: what does
my foe need to be my friend? Resilience
means you need not win, and yet prevail.

Raccoon in Plum Time

You live in a hollow tree—with bugs. In rain,
you drag heavy—coat and tail soggy where
streetlights glitter. You watch your paws
soften scraps in muddy puddles, making do
with what you find—peel, bone, rind.
Every street could be your last—headlights
hunting you flat. Then dogs—send you up a tree
for laughs, they'll sit there bragging as if they're
wolves. And you can only steal so much
cat food, scattered stinking underfoot before
you gag. What's abundance, if it's vile?

But then September, big moon, and your prowling
finds the plums dropping in heaps so sweet and fat
you stagger deep, whiskers quivering to lick, suck,
gnash, and swallow until you're sticky, lolling tipsy,
bandit happy, lusty gusto, shaky elbow, roly poly
on your side helpless with joy.

All those rainy nights of cold to come—
you'll remember plum time.

Regeneration Parable

On wind a seed with feather crown, a bead
bristling with legacy for life, born to lift its gift
went drifting, seeking, sifting slot and crevice—
not this road without a crack, not this crack without
damp, but this seam in concrete wet and yearning
for a root thread the seed sent fingering, lingering, loving
ever deeper into dense dark. And up went the green flag
flickering, shred of living light bedded in this broken world.

So I say unto you be not afraid, no matter how small
your poor power against the powers that be, no worry
your wan wit against wanton greed, no fear your
fragile force against any fever that claims the name
of progress as it wages war against the earth. Be
the seed where you are, so small they don't see you
coming, so weak you don't give warning, so
persistent they can't protect the geologic castle

from the green, the young, the generation of the new.
Life's in for the long game, the strong change
by the many and the small. All of us in one circle
wider than division, earth-round circumference
flowing, shifting, growing, greening, shining,
reaching, breaching, seeking, waking, wondering,
wandering, winding, rooting, vining, veering,
vanishing, then winging, singing, bringing
with feathered crown a seed.

To My Hand the River
Offers Rounded Stones

Fish fit every sleeve of water.
Here the cottonwood is making perfect leaves.
Wren song flies in all directions—no impediment.
Clover nectar welcomes tongues of bees.
How can I be stingy here in heaven
where our covenant is clear?
The river brims with woven rain.
Wind is whispering the trees.

The Big Empty

Some go to the sea so their gaze
may venture far, unencumbered
by roads or plans. Walking the tideline,
they face wild essence of salt.

Some prefer mountains, a hut
at road's end where forest stretches
unbroken to the peaks, so they can study
a puzzle of twig, moss, and rivulet.

These are mystified by those
who live in cities, in rooms, in cells
on arteries of asphalt, skies tangled
with wires, thought in gridlock.

I need the big empty east of the mountains,
please—by night the next light on horizon's
hoop distant as a star. Give me the playa
where I can walk blind to be lost and lucky.

Lightning, Thunder, Rain

When clouds bring their dark lid low and air
stinks of burnt rain, when sighing leaves shift
and seethe, when trees grip earth for life, bracing
for the gusty flail, when shadowed birds flee
to thickets for the first crack and clap, all wisp
of science flies fugitive from mind, stripped bodies
naked of knowledge, stunted into sudden childhood
dressed in a sheath of myth again, broken back to origin
before the blinding sizzle boom and rush of rain.
What was a tree is smoking splinters, what was our
certainty is all in ruins, so we sing glory, glory, glory.

Your Animal

Speaking of the birds and bees,
do you like to horse around, be the dark
horse, see a man about a horse, drink
like a fish, get all squirrely?
Or do you avoid the goose step
and travel at a snail's pace? Do you
have a cow, then feel sheepish? Are
you the monkey's uncle, for monkey
business, busy bee, busy beaver
in the rat-race that makes you dog-tired
by night? Or are you a night owl, an old
dinosaur? Can you be catty, a jaybird,
gossip, or do you clam up, mourning dove
eating crow? Are you some mousy type,
who can be a real bear sometimes,
ratting on your friends, ferreting
out their secrets, crowing trouble?
In your family, are you the black sheep,
the lamb led to slaughter, the scapegoat?
Or are you the elephant in the room?
If you think about it—it's a zoo.
But what can you do? You're a chicken
when it comes to fessing up, bug-eyed
in the mirror, seeing a real fox, then
lipstick on a pig, an ugly duckling, one
lone wolf lovebird—or do you simply
put your head in the sand and wonder
who you really are?

Water Song

I flow lower, slower, sliding wet in rivulet
or defile, creep deep, seep under, sift through,
turn blue, mist up from wave or pool, fool
to be gone, abscond beyond accountability,
myriad molecule sipped by Caesar, fog
furrowing battlefields, shining shields,
surrender's yield sealed sacred, feeling
my way from thicket or conflict,
healing drought, pouring out, ooze from
wounds, sound of splash, blood from lash,
river's dash from peak to sea, pleased
to meet you, travel through you, lost ghost
in your shape, rain cape descending,
sending my battalions over islands,
storm stallions stamping feet of lace,
dawn song, small saint, clear paint,
face dressed, soul blessed, best taste,
not much, a healing touch, and gone.

Calypso Lily

Thumb-size dusky purple cradle
on a hand-span grass-thin stem
under old trees, hard to see from above,
but from the airy ground-hugging saunter
of bumblebees a shock of yellow tuft
and fleshy cave where sufficient pollen
dusted by bee fur from a fellow flower
may engender 20,000 seeds for big hope
of a small blossom easily trampled, almost
invisible in the gloom of ancient groves.

When fire comes, stem's gone, leaf
a ghost of ash, but the corm in mycorrhizal
fungi alive by root filaments sipping
old rain hoarded under stones.

Named for a greedy lover in the old
Greek tale, island girl who snared
her wanderer to bed him in her cave,
to wear him out with ecstasy, longing
to make him immortal—forest flower
dug by eager gardeners doomed to fail,
for Calypso needs protection by old trees
and old-tree earth, shadow heaven
of sustained decay.

Fairy slipper, deer-head flower,
whose one leaf grows in autumn,
overwinters, then withers with summer
so there is nothing to be seen of her
but dun old-growth litter of her home—

How the Crow Knows Her Love

He has a certain swagger in the way he dips his beak,
a syncopated strutting when he gives a tender shriek.
I meet him in the shadows to tickle at his chin, to preen
his glossy feathers, till he shivers deep within. For I know
behind his swagger he's a blooming fool for love. I can
make him coo with pleasure as if he were a dove. I can
make his vision blur, his eyes roll back and blink, and
remind him of this later when I give a fetching wink.
He makes me swoon with wonder when he flaps
across the sun to bring me fragrant morsels, and
I know that he's the one—the one to raise our crowlets,
teach them verve and zest, so they can swagger like him
by the time they leave the nest. Oh I can pick him
from the flock, be they thousands in the trees—he
makes my heart beat faster and go weak in wings and knees.
When he glances past his shoulder to give that sassy look,
I know I've got his number—I can read him like a rook.
But how these humans find each other is an ancient mystery,
for swarming in their flocks they're all look-alikes to me.
No inky feet and feathers with rainbow hue to spy—the one
who has that swagger that can always catch my eye. How they
find their partners is a thing nobody knows. It's a pleasure
that's so easy when you live among the crows.

Symbiosis

In high school, it was a concept—
two organisms helping one another,
a vocab word on the bio quiz
with extra credit if you could tell
about *lichen* (Greek, "one that licks"),
the meshed marriage of algae
and fungus living as one
for mutual benefit, crusting
rock, surviving on rain and dust
in Arctic or Sahara, holding
a sweet spot between the parasitic
and the independent.

Now I watch this concept grow
to embrace our entire project
of life on Earth, where all creatures
may survive only by this kind of marriage,
kinship, family, tribe, where we
are all one crust living on stone.

Light in Earth

The physiological and ecological
function of fungal bioluminescence
has not been established
with certainty.

After dusk, when full dark descends,
step into the forest without your light
to seek the light you find: not
starlight high, no mechanical
shine by human cleverness, but
lit fungi firing up their green
glow from gloom.

From the lineage of *Omphalotus*,
from the lineage of *Neonothopanus*,
from *Armillaria* and *Mycenoid*, from
the newly named *Lucentipes* lineage
begin to see fungi seeding light in darkness,
bioluminescent forest denizens with lit spores
ferrying their lanterns on wind to spawn
tiny twinkling kingdoms, to send their filaments
illuminate into earth, carving darkness into lace.

Eager everywhere, tendrils dig their fire
into duff and down, fabric embroidered
with dusty luminescence deep in earth,
blunt tip of each thread probing darkness,
the miner's lamp of life seeking to sip
mineral clay through all interstices
into collective resonance.

You'll need the dark to see. You'll need
humility. Without not knowing how it works,
how can you apprehend such silence,
such soft efficiency everywhere in earth,
your smudge-lit finger reaching down
to touch the fruiting body damp and cold
with ancient boundless vigor?

Horses of Iceland

Islenski Hesturinn

Deep in the dark age when Vikings chose
which breed to board their ships for Iceland,
none but tough would do, no more than
fourteen hands in height, sure-footed
for broken ground, born with a gait
for every obstacle, an easy keeper, sturdy
in winter, yet warm, kind, holding kinship
with human touch, a horse to stand on deck
fearless as waves heave and wind shrieks,
bold in storm yet ready from myth and saga
to step down the slope to meet us yesterday,
curious to nibble our sleeves, this herd of twenty
crowding closer all around us, noses needing rub
and scratch, chins lifted for any touch we might
return by the old covenant between their kind
and some Viking in us yet, asking with
their eyes and turn of head: are you
with us wherever we may venture?

Under My Breath

As I strayed before dawn
the white hot full moon
punched me in the eye,
and tall stars slid
their needles into my
upraised arms praising
what hurt, as crickets
chanted psalms from shadows
so ravishing in small I had to
whisper with them, be their animal,
and silence pouring from the dark
ravine hit me like a wave
deafening my defenses
until I was a rag.

All these earth beauties
hammering my heart, is it
any wonder I can't live forever
if such pleasures bruise me
every night?

On the Beaten Path

There's something to be said for common ways
and I'm going to say it: if the road most taken
means earning my bread by the sweat of my brow,
I'm on it. If it means trustworthy kinship, I'm for it.
If my path is beaten flat by parents loving their almost
impossible work of raising the future, I say yes.
If it means long good beyond my time, yes.
If it requires living within our means,
I sing praise for ordinary life.

But if it means same old same old business as usual
war against earth, theft of our children's future, lies
for gain by top-down leaders leading us to hell,
I'm off that road—aren't you? If it means blind
leading blind, same old dirge of our limitations
falling on deaf ears, logical outcome looming
in terrors on the horizon for our mindless parade,
let's turn aside on foot, here where deer made a path
threading the thicket to an open field.

Why I Became an Earth Dweller

Because at four I danced from the wood with snakes
ringing my wrists. Because I took my pillow to sleep
with rabbits in their straw. Because doves in shadow
had a call that tugged. Because ladybugs turned crimson
on my fingertips, clapped open their wings, and flew.
Because I found half an arrowhead of clear obsidian,
and peering through it could see ancient smoky sky.
Because an ouzel plunged from her mossy nest
into whitewater foam. Because the blue scorpion
raised a stinger when I pried open a rotten stump.
Because flipping creek stones, I could watch
muddy water clear, then snatch feisty crawdads
behind their claws. Because I could smell cedar sap
on my hands in school. Because dawn spiderwebs
across my path meant no one was there before me.
Because dry hemlock twigs could kindle my tiny fire,
I could fall asleep beside it, and all my life wake
to breathe on the embers and rouse a new flame.

Inventory of Light

I remember a cherry tree with blossoms shivering
through glass over my bed, buried in its light.
I remember a cross through my tears when I was
bad, sent to my darkness, staring up at streetlight.
I remember lightning in wheat fields at midnight,
wandering feral at age twelve, that ball of fire
swinging before my face, terror thrusting my hand
into my mouth. I remember speckled shadows
in spangling alder thickets at Ninilchik where I whittled
a little cougar for my sister, slinking forepaw raised.
I remember a butter lamp's flicker at Tiger's Nest
where I wept for my brother . . . crisp moon
slicing waves at Moran where I shipped my oars,
curled in the prow, and slept . . . that low gold
over dusty roads to Hermosillo telling a different
story than the one I lived . . . first light seeping
into the forest at Subasio where brother sun
courted my spirit, and I said yes. There were
always people, jobs, calendar days, the mesh
of money and duty, saving and spending, sorrow
and joy—but outside all that, light hinting,
offering, summoning, asking if I was ready
to be other, asking if I was brave.

Birding for the Blind

Without any clutter of color, wing bar, breast-band,
of eyeline, or cap, without binoculars dangling or
field guide flopped open, but standing spare in the open,
you turn your head to hear a clear yodel, whistle, trill,
fuzzy tremolo, falling flute of a dark minor third—
in the thicket someone calling *hey sweetie, hey sweetie* so
you step closer, with your stick and hunger, as someone else
says *cooks for you, cooks for you* which makes you turn
to the wind's direction to hear *whichity whichity whichity*,
some arpeggio of joy, some Mozart of this meadow, some
Chopin in the hedgerow, some lost love calling you to kneel,
to fumble together a nest of grass, cupped with thistledown.

Woman Pumping Gas
Tells Me about Her Crows

Through her pandemic mask, she confirms,
"Fill it? Regular? No receipt?" As her left hand
spins off the gas cap, her right slides home
the nozzle, and with a click the flow hums.

"See them?" She cocks her head to the power line,
where one crow hunches, cries, another flaps
and settles, turns in place, shrugs, steps closer.
"That's her baby calling, not yet learned to fly."

Above the mask, her eyes look far. "I watched
all through June, July. Something got the others.
That one's left." We both look up at two silhouettes
against the sky. The gas sings. The young crow cries.

"My own girl's still home. Grown, but not gone.
Crow mama taught me: Give her time."
The gas valve clicks off. She holsters
the nozzle, spins tight the cap.

"You said no receipt?"

Crow on the Cross

Tecolote de guadaña,
pájaro madrugador . . .

After agony's over—weeping mother
gone to rest . . . nails pulled, wiped clean,
saved to build a stable . . . crown of thorns
become a hawk's nest . . . spilled blood
nourishing lilies—a crow finds her
sturdy perch, songbirds sing from battlefield
barbwire, doves murmur from pines grown tall
in empty prison yards, and owls hunch
in silhouette along the border wall.

After Fire, Rain

Soft smoke of hard rain
drills down through tree bones.
Hiss and steam of quenched fire—
rain nips flame's root, gray mud of ash.
Rain walks up the canyon, reaching down
for every stem reaching up, dressing wounds.
Sound of rain slaps your hat. Rain gloves grip.
Rain makes your coat heavy, your bare neck chill.
Boots print mud, leave simple signatures of rain.
Rain washes what was seared, culled, fallen, lost.
Where fire starved, rain gives rest and restoration.

Rain turns eye-salt to rivulets, rivulets
to rivers wheresoever many weep as one.
After fire, rain offers a few true words.
Rain thrusts deep in earth, seeking seeds.
Rain in haste, eager rain, patient rain,
rain taking its own sweet time.
Earth's thirst for first rain—
never to be cursed again.

Out Oak Island Road

for Steve Wilson

In swales and furrows, low-slung fields
fill with rain for channel, pool, pond, and
down came cranes, swans, geese in flocks wheeling,
calling, veering to a stall to settle muttering in their
restless multitudes, all ruffle and strut, feeding,
preening, dancing, drifting in their radiance that
brought me closer, stepping, stopping, gazing, gasping
at their finery, stunned by their numbers, vast bounty
of beauty in their wild and ancient abundance, owning
earth before any human claim—until I came too close
and they beat upward, clamoring, stammering, hammering
air with their singing wings, calling down my name
in shame, and all our names to one another as they
billowed up, filled the sky, then left it empty.

Why the Beach?

for Sheryl & Janet

Half the horizon—ancient: no wires, no roads, no
development. Maybe a boat out there tracing lonesome.
Waves roar their heartbeat whispers. People have come
here to be here, so they walk barefoot, like children.
Children run wild. Weather rules it all. Something
bigger is in charge of you. And every night, she
reasserts her sovereignty. And every night, she
cleans up. Yesterday's tracks are gone, even
that dance of a dog's joy. Lots of soaring going on—
gulls, crows, pelicans, maybe a kite, maybe your gaze,
your spirit spiraling the sky. Each day, an old man
walks to pick up litter. Each day an old woman walks
to find the perfect stone. You can walk without a plan.
You can sing with wind. You can cry in peace. You can
remember being small. You can be small beside immensity.
You can be the simple you. For when you said,
"I'm going to the beach," no one said, "Why?"

Wood Too Good to Cut

Under the porch, this cedar plank,
impossibly wide, thick as my fist—
this one Curtis gave when he retired.
First I must build a room worthy
of the table it could be.

Behind the house, this redwood post
I pulled from the dump at Metolius
leans under the northside eave,
honored long in fragrant shade,
still standing as a sacred tree.

And this bolt of yew I cut north
from Fish Lake, bowing in the grove
with my folding saw, old snow still
on the ground around me, so my father
could make a bow, but then he died.

I need to be a boy again standing
at his knee before he can split it
with his hatchet from the war, then
shave it to a stave, gripping his
shattered knuckle of glass.

Stranger in the House

I was a stranger in the house of Earth—
broke the door, insulted the family,
never learned the language
beyond *want ... mine ... now ...* ,
slept in the best room, scattered
my debris, kicked the dog,
never fed the cat, threw out
the children's toys.

Once I was gone, they all
looked at each other, surveyed
the damage—sheen of oil, bones
of whales, dusty drought. They
shook their heads, and someone
said, "What was that about?"

Runes of the Ancients

After the Great Catastrophe, the Ancients
left marks scratched on stone and bone
our shamans begin to interpret only now:

=	Sky above, Earth below.
+	One stands alone on Earth.
#	Two stand together on Earth.
////	Counted by hand, enough.
~	A young river.
$	Following a river.
()	Hidden by day.
*	Seen by starlight.
!	A raindrop's path.
&	Knot of memory.
@	Safe at home.
%	Blind on Earth.

What can we learn from their struggles?
How can we dodge their fate?

The Monkish Habits of Trees

Cleave wood and I am there.
—Gospel of St. Thomas

Stand apart, but in community.
Wake by the clock of cold stars.
Chant the hours for the sky.
Live by the Rule, labor in silence,
delve in your garden enclosed.
Remember: "to work is to pray."
Lose your self in contemplation.
Give your whole soul to prayer.
Believe in many miracles.
Remember St. Oak & St. Ash.
Honor their feast days.
Welcome strangers as holy beings.
Make beautiful books, leaf by leaf.
Offer good news to all.
Open your arms in praise.
The kingdom is within you.

Earth Appoints a Child
to Make the Case

You guys are all dressed up! Is this your
dinner table? It's really big. Okay, so—
I was down in the woods near my house
minding my own business, but this voice
out of nowhere starts talking, talking to me,
starts teaching me this big word: *"non-neg...*
non-negosh... negosh... non-negotiable."
That's it. This change that's coming is
non-negotiable. That's the whole thing
I'm supposed to tell you guys. The voice
said you don't seem to know that. Then it
went away, and I stood there in the trees.
So that's it, okay? The big change is just
non-negotiable. Now can I get on my bike
and go home? My mom will kill me if I'm late.

Moss Offers

If you let us luxuriate on fallen houses
that loomed their misty gloom before our spores
poured golden into sunlit spindles rising in a dance
to dress all human contraptions in their time of grandeur,
preparing for their fall;

and if green in dusky shadows could be concrete's
soft salvation, could gild each seam with damp to be
moonlight's cushion, to be fur of earth, feathered
hunch, hint and promise, silent singing
prophecy of dawn;

and if for cities we could be a restoration principle,
repair for broken covenants, teaching how to humble
them new, burrow through tattered certainties
to wake seeds, sprouts, and buds of life's
most honest longing;

then we could redeem your ways of subjugation,
gather green light born from gray, mantle every
monument, blanket streets for your soft tread
from spring to shelter, usher in old ways of Eden
long vivid in your dreams.

Hut of the Palace Builder

Near the hilltop construction site, hurly burly
with stacks of stone, timbers hewn and marked
for puzzling together into vast halls and chilly galleries—

in a ravine below, shadowed by hazel and wild plum,
where birds flit from twigs to gather grasses for their
simple basket cradles, in that thicket sits the builder's hut

that will stand a few seasons, when dusk is a treasure and sleep
is easy (a bucket from the spring, a loaf from the fire, butterfly
alighting on a rough hand held forth in sunlight) . . .

then the hut's left empty when construction's done, birds
thieving thatch, and bees hiving the hollow wall, a badger
denned under rejected blocks of stone in their heap . . .

until the hut is found by palace children bored by grandeur,
now playing house at the peasant's table, gathering berries
in a cracked bowl, singing with the wild birds.

Track of the Young Crane

for Guthrie at 24

We paddled to the swamp when the lake
was low, dragged our canoe through shallows,
stepped onto the mudflat to scatter, seeking toad
and feather, cattail, yellow lily, each intent to find
what beckoned from the old wild world. Geese
guarded the water far, a deer peered from shadows,
muskrat tunneled in ancient mud. Then you called
me close to see tracks of sandhill cranes, young
among their elders crisscross at the water's edge—
and we heard them calling from willows west,
their chortle rattle syllable of yes. And I say yes
to you, yes to this miracle of being, no matter
what we are called to do, yes and yes in smoke
and change, in a world that needs our yes
empowered by clear seeing, seeking,
wondering, wandering, buoyant, curious,
ready, thoughtful, eager to gaze in all
directions, turning as I did to see
your barefoot track by mine.

In Spirit

After, you will find me here.
No freight of bone or sorrow, I can sail
where hawks ride, raven pair in wind.
Where now only my gaze can trace
the playa's perimeter, roving its long
circumference rim to rim, in spirit I will
drift for loving investigation to every stem
that rises green to sway, to wither gold, and go,
put my ear to every stone to know its lineage,
nibble every rose hip wrinkle, study every
old leaf turned to lace, every trace of beetle
in dust, every starlight print stamped in mud.
I can whisper to make them weep walking out
through blowing snow to the big empty. I can
offer hunch, hint, and trance epiphany—
humming swarm of beauties that haunt
the living here. First light east, last light west,
rind of illumination cresting, waning,
seeping underground—that will be my
yearning matured to ordinary magic.
When geese come north, and cranes
toss their sticks and dance, when
tufted singers flit to bend their willow
wands in singing ecstasy, when moth
follows moon, when sage blooms
and cottonwood swivels little leaves,
I'll travel like scent or shimmer here,
wind ripple through grass.
Watch for me then.

2.

Plum Trees in War

American Crazy Quilt

To stitch together old glory right
for these times that try men's souls some
blues Betsy might piece choice scraps, like
I cannot tell a lie about the melting pot
to set beside John Henry's hammer ringing
twinkle, twinkle little bombs bursting in air,
where oh say can you see, oh beautiful
for spacious operation enduring freedom
is a mission accomplished after Enola Gay's
day of infamy over there is why we hold
these truths to be as long as the rivers shall run,
as in many one homeland security our great
national nightmare has been lynched, and
the only good Indian reservation system
boarding schools taught the golden spike
as manifest destiny, because the sea of buffalo
homestead act planted the flag in the woods
are lovely dark doodle dandy veteran sang
my old Kentucky to mean ask not what mine
eyes have seen the glory of the separate but
equal right to choose our trespasses frankly,
my dear, the plums were so sweet, but if you
can't lick 'em join the mob to survive the great
depression, even though roses are red, violets
are blue in the pursuit of happiness Hollywood
is the only thing to fear shall yet endure.

So Still

a song for vigil

They took Eric for a cigarette.
They took George for a twenty dollar bill.
Breonna is gone 'cause they didn't like
her door. Who will be the next to lie so still?

They took Ahmaud for running.
They took Laquan because he walked
away. They took Trayvon 'cause he was
lookin' 'round. Wrong time, wrong place,
is all they say.

They took Emmett for a whistle.
They took Medgar for a word.
They took Martin 'cause they didn't like
his dream. Again, they said, it's time
that dream's deferred.

So still, did they kill you for a thrill?
So still, in your casket,
so silent, and so chill.
They took away your laughter,
let us keep our tears.

They took you in your troubles,
in your tender years. They took you
for your color, that's how it appears.
And when will we decide true justice
to fulfill, before we let another
                              lie so still?

The Fauci-Trump Scale
of Human Character

1. Seeing a child weeping alone, would you:
   a. bow close to ask what's wrong . . .
   b. shout for the parents . . .
   c. call ICE.

2. Seeing hospitals filled by Covid, would you:
   a. address the community about how to help . . .
   b. briskly walk away . . .
   c. pout.

3. Seeing facts that contradict your hopes,
   would you:
   a. learn . . .
   b. malinger . . .
   c. lie.

4. Seeing you have failed to achieve
   your cherished outcome, would you:
   a. confess your failure . . .
   b. spin the story . . .
   c. golf.

Shakespeare Gives No Call-Back to an Aging Actor

Thou hath vice and villainy, rich and plenty.
Thou canst strut and fret as a crow at carrion,
or a mewling child denied. I could see thee
as a man of walls and towers, haughty in reserve,
a terror to maids and suckling babes. But thy speech
is twittering, thy pride barren. Thy heart hungers vainly
for that villainous pallor I could fashion to fright
groundlings groveling for thy scraps of anguish,
and also chill those dressed in lace and scarlet fine.
Alas, thy posturings are hollow, thy ravings crowded
thick with shallow words. Thou art no Macbeth
or Lear, couldst not rise to a singing rage, nor go mad
and wander pelted by a storm of sorrows. For all
thy promise, thou couldst not drive my quill, spattering
in fevered haste to pin thee living to the page.

But be not downcast. Have this life. I'll leave thee
with this consolation small: in some speech, perhaps,
rolling from the tongue of a swaggerer, thou shalt be a tale
told swiftly of one who had his brittle time in power, who
would be king, but then was found to be a man.
Savor thy dignity in this, and act well thy part.

The Cardinal Debates the Jay

Cardinal perched crimson
on the topmost branch of a twisted
pine, Bluejay on a twig below,
as they both fluffed their feathers.

"This top branch is mine to keep,"
Cardinal said—"your riffraff
flock can't change that. And if
they try, we'll ask the owls."

"I believe in long migration,"
Bluejay said—"in a different
season coming. Have you given
no thought to the fledglings?"

"You and your far horizon,"
Cardinal cried. "I believe
in this branch now—so beautiful!
Everything else—rumors and lies."

"Look down," Bluejay said. "Oh
say can you see the sparrow, towhee,
nuthatch, flicker, heron, thrasher, swan,
the raven, crow, the robin and the wren?"

Fire Sale in D.C.

Everything must go—the lies, rumors,
proclamations, dog-whistle hints. No more
walls and towers, no more hush money,
no more claims swiveling like weather vanes.

Rock bottom—no more rallies railing about
the old swamp in the new swamp. No more
innuendos tailored to proud boys. No more
"I'll be with you" before late-night TV.

Take it down to the bare walls—no more
photo ops, sharpies. No executions
for the unlucky, pardons for the guilty.
No more drilling the pristine.
No more kidnapping children.

No more flimsy flouting, flaunting, flubbing,
flattering, fluffing, fleecing, floundering
while the world turns, while skies burn,
while storms churn, while the young yearn.

D.C. Weather Report

The cold front that arrived some years ago
shows signs of breaking up in the coming weeks
as a new weather system moving in from all directions
has gathered in tornado alley and the Bible belt,
where the clouds have parted, and visibility improved.
This generally happens when the barometer drops
and stale air is freshened by incoming winds. Stubbornly,
the storm's eye remains fixed in the oval office, where
observers have noted an air of preternatural calm
that long-time weather watchers know can be fickle.
Throughout the country, local residents are still repairing
storm damage from previous events, from fires creating
their own weather, from drought, from wind-shear episodes
of Stormy Daniels, ICE, Sharpiegate, and a surge of evictions
despite the fabled Operation Warp Speed. At least for now,
Hurricane Melania remains stalled off the coast, but may
make landfall soon, though evacuation orders have been
put on hold. Stay tuned. As you can see by our satellite
weather map, when viewed from above the whole country
is gripped by unsettled conditions, shifting trends, where
from California to the Gulf Stream waters, this land
is due for atmospheric change. Forecast: windy
late in the day, with an overnight low.

Joint Session of Congress

After a few tokes, it all began to change—
Mitch cracked a joke from the Kentucky hills
to break the ice, and Chuck told his version
from the Catskills that made everyone
hoot and holler. Blue smoke rose and
someone flicked on the disco light that
made Ted, singing a *corrido* he'd learned
in Laredo, become a harmless uncle, and
that made Marco cry, as Nancy got them all
in order to learn her favorite line dance:
Boy-Girl-Boy-Girl, she called out with a giggle,
as from the gallery the Marine Band poured down
New Orleans jazz, and they all let the good times roll.

The Moth Vote

No more streetlights! (Let them all go dark).
We will have the moon. The minnow vote:
No more herons! *We will glitter free.*
Rivers agree: *Go around the opposition.*
Butterflies in solidarity: *Don't pin us down.*
Skunk's campaign slogan: *It makes scents.*
The race for top turtle got off to a slow start:
Easy does it. In the possum campaign, scandal
got no traction: *We all sleep around.* Nail-biter?
Cliff-hanger, dead-heat, re-count run-off?
That's the law of tooth and claw. But in
the end, mud won by a landslide.

Nurse's Note

When it began, you called us heroes—for facing down
the scourge, short on masks but long on pluck
to honor every life from admitting to last breath.
You sang to us, you honked and spread our portraits
in the news just for doing our jobs.

You sang, yes, but you didn't change—instead,
by a rising epidemic of denial (you couldn't
mask, stay home, get vaccinated, or forgo your
festive habits of wandering for pleasure),
we were finally overwhelmed.

Look into my eyes so I know you hear me.
You made us choose: give up our calling or be
stricken on the job and die, leaving our children
weeping, alone, bitter with stories
of your fatal nonchalance.

Second Shot

At the pharmacy, waiting my turn
in the aisle of greeting cards—between
"Get Well Soon" and "Son/Birthday/Funny"—
I love the old lady bowing over her older mother
crumpled into a chair. I love the frumpy codger
in robe and slippers. I love the feeble couple
leaning together like trees. I love the athlete dressed
for running and bantering with strangers. I love
"Is this the line? . . . Are you next? . . . Take my seat."
And oh how I love the pharmacist, Asian American
in white coat, blue gloves, babbling about his
parents, still safe, but far—as he so deftly jabs
my eager arm, and I rise under fluorescence
to thread my way through this lovely world.

The Supremes

They used to be so great—that string of hits
in the fifties, sixties, seventies? Off the charts.
Their work set a precedent others followed.
When they got unanimous, their harmonies
changed us. You felt a hum everywhere
that came from them. A new kind of freedom
flowed over the land. That one about kids
in school, the one about woman power.
Holy moly, when they held court, they were
on a roll. You didn't need anyone's judgment call—
they were tops. But I guess it couldn't last. They
got some new blood, started doing covers by
splinter groups, lost their mojo. Some died,
some went solo. You couldn't really call them
The Supremes any more. They stopped setting
the beat. No more anthems, just echoes.

Headline

Retired Priest Performs Last Rites for Possum
on Highway, then Creature Revives Restoring
Faith of Family Who Stopped to Watch, Leading
Children Years Later to Study Zoology and Spend
Career Preserving Habitat for Endangered Species,
Working in Collaboration with Local Residents,
Resulting in Advocacy for Rural Poor Starting
with Access to Clean Water as Constitutional
Amendment for First Right of All Children,
with Effort Joining Demonstrations in Cities
Chanting I Can't Breathe and Holding Up
Chalices Filled with Rain, Causing Police
Chief to Remember Grandmother's Last
Wish that He Become a Teacher, Causing
Order to Desist Confrontation and Begin
Dialog, as Protesters Distribute Counterfeit
Twenty Dollar Bills with Image of George
Floyd and Motto *E Pluribus Pluribus* as
First Step toward Democracy of True
Inclusion in All Matters of Grace.

This Conversation May Be Recorded
for Quality Assurance

I'm glad somebody cares
when I call customer service
to ask about my last billing cycle, and
get a woman in India with a lovely accent,
her voice freighted by satellite to sort
my payment: "How can I help you?"

And after we delve into enigma, beyond
our conversation, somewhere later, far away,
someone else prepares to listen, for quality
assurance, perhaps a mother in North Carolina
trying to make ends meet, or an immigrant
in Chicago moonlighting to send money home.

Think of it—we send our voices to mingle
out there beyond this great emptiness, speaking
our oldest human contract—"Can I help?" . . .
and then, alert to the timbre of a human voice,
someone attends to how certain syllables may assure
the quality of our essential bond.

Night Flight of the Screaming Child

She's onto something, she knows what's ahead,
so her sorrow aria rises, her wail of woe for this infinite
red-eye drive through dense dark, for our headwind shudder
tuned to her tiny piercing shriek that bellows and billows
wider as we ascend to cruising. Why are we all so intent
on torturing her like this, belting her taut for the long haul
roaring over a ruined world to convey her little life
toward a tragic dawn?

In the Children We Will Make Our Home

a pantoum for new citizens

In the children we will make our home
With food, and songs, and stories.
Many treasures we have left behind,
Always loyal to the future.

With food, and songs, and stories,
With hands, with feet, with listening,
Always loyal to the future—
Sometimes with words others do not know . . .

With hands, with feet, with listening,
Under sun, and moon, and stars—
Sometimes with words others do not know,
Now as many we are one.

Under sun, and moon, and stars,
Many treasures we have left behind.
Now as many we are one.
In the children we will make our home.

Sometimes with words others do not know,
With food, and songs, and stories—
Always loyal to the future,
Now as many we are one.

Museum on Fire

Captions burn first—wafers on pins.
Then all artifacts of lace rush into ash,
the spinner's craft, frocks and ribbons gone.
Wood goes, then bone, until only stone
still reveals how water spirals and swirls
as someone chiseled it into a slab, a grave
stone or sacrificial table lost, centuries buried,
to be dug from the bog, washed, mounted here.

It's hot, smoke makes it hard to see, and the streets
are clogged with useless wrecks. This time there are
no exits, only the labyrinth of the city as it was,
all its small glories and mysteries blurred by fire.
So why am I still writing this caption, trying
to explain the meaning of all we have made
and been, while our story rises into flames
and all that was beautiful . . .

Mother Russia, Wounded
by the Modern Tsar

Why are boys dressed in drab and given guns?
Sparrows peck spilled grain.

Why is steel the color of choice?
Crows haunt smoky fields.

Why does grandfather let his tea grow cold?
Frost gripped sprouting wheat.

How much rain to fill the Volga?
Not soon, the end of weeping.

Late snow at Zima Junction.
Which ravine will hold the bones?

Leningrad, 2022

Somewhere in Mariupol, on the Sea of Azov,
where Tatars plundered, then Norgay hordes made
slave raids, then Ottomans ruled the desolate steppe,
then Cossacks camped, now under Russian siege
amid library rubble a book lies open, smoke fingering
its pages to find Hitler's order for Leningrad in 1941:

> *Following the city's encirclement, requests*
> *for surrender negotiations shall be denied,*
> *since the problem of relocating and feeding*
> *the population cannot and should not be solved*
> *by us. In this war for our very existence, we*
> *can have no interest in maintaining even*
> *a part of this very large urban population.*

Banners of smoke, a single shoe, no brick's left on brick—
but a book remembers what tyrants forget.

The Hard Part

It's easy to lie, at first.
People want to believe you.
And betrayal—a cinch.
You control the first move.
Killing is so easy, it's absurd.
People didn't see it coming.
Even war, if you're the one
to start it, goes well for a while.
Sure, people hate you, fear you,
looking down as they surrender.
Once you win, for a thin moment
you enjoy that ornate word: Victory.
It glitters in your hands like dirty gold.

Calling Home

How can we kill them—they look like us.
—soldier in Ukraine

An old man, who limped like uncle Alexi, stumbled,
and we shot him. He had a gun, yes, but he wore a cap
like the one you knit for me. One wore a coat like father's,
we shot him off a bridge into the river. When I shot one running
into the forest, his hands flew up like brother Oleg, twitching.
I remember grandfather Sasha shouting when he was disturbed
too early, before his tea. Here a graybeard shouted as we passed,
and my commander shot him on his doorstep. One my age, when he
was hit, cried out "Arina!" Who will have to tell her? If I die,
who will tell you? I can't sleep—I see these faces everywhere.
When my gun is cold, I am afraid. When it is hot, I am ashamed.
What will happen to children here, like our Slava, our Ksenia?
And if I live, after I have a hero's welcome, tell me, mother,
after you hold me in your arms, what will happen to me?

Chaos Theory

Can a butterfly, flexing her wings
on battlefields, birth a storm to pelt
the Tsar's palace windows and cause him
to remember his grandmother's soft hands
so tender with his young fear he calls
the troops home? No, you say? How can
you be so sure? Just because it hasn't
happened yet, do you think this moth
on a soldier's fingertip on night watch
under the full moon, stirred by his
frighted breath just before the signal
to attack, shouldn't try again?

Chain of Command

If you are a young soldier on night watch guarding
some great engine of steel hunched in a snowy field—
a tank, say, or rocket-launcher—as you stare far into
vicious mirk, you command only your finger on a cold
trigger as your wide eyes play tricks with shifting
smudges out there yearning to shoot you, bathe your
body in fire, strip life from your bones in all the nightmare
scenarios that crowd your mind—you are controlled
by your CO sleeping in a farmhouse back behind the trees,
who is controlled by a general in a dacha down the road,
who is controlled by a tyrant in a palace to the east,
whose hands and feet twitch, plucked by strings
of the puppet master, that grand idea of empire
hovering in glory somewhere just above. But for you,
it's only the half-moon high, and just out of sight,
across the field, your death, coming.

Walking on the Dead

They chose my field, and after the backhoe gashed
a ditch two farmers deep, they called me from the house
to help swing bodies from the truck—some wrapped
in sheets, curtains, or just their coats. They fell side by side,
but some got jumbled, and when the next truck came,
they told me to get down in there and straighten things.

One red shoe. A torn lapel. A beard. A ponytail.
A hand gloved in soot. A cheek with lipstick, or blood.
Each step, suck, and crack. Dizzy terror stench.

Don't ask me how children take little space, how
a pregnant mother must be on her side. Don't make me tell
how my weeping broke for slime sunk to ooze into the voids.
Don't ask about their faces in my dreams, begging why
this is a country, instead of a simple place under the sky.
And from this field, make no one eat bread.

Blue

Uncle brought it from his journey
to give for the shine in mother's eyes,
to put in our window so anyone
walking the dirt road of our village
could see like a jewel the blue vase
people in Ukraine gave him in gratitude
for trying to free them from oppression,
even though he came home hungry, his
uniform torn, his shoes coming apart, but
in his bag this glass that gleamed more bright
with light than anyone had ever seen, more
like the sky when it is heaven. Someday,
I told him, I will go there. But he said
nothing, only put his hand on my head,
then stroked the cow's neck as she grazed
in our yard, as he looked far to the west.

Beyond This War

Stumbling on level ground, like a tired
grandfather grown clumsy, grown forgetful,
a war, too, must falter and die. Already it grows
old, and its time will come. Trees now, though
they lost limbs splintered in the fighting, begin
to seal their wounds, and muttering crows, hiding
for now in the forest, have begun to plan their return.
Children who stayed away from windows, and slept
in their clothes, ready to run—children who now
remember war starting, someday will remember
how it ended, how people poured into the streets,
shouting and singing, and the pleasures of ordinary
days returned at last. For now, yes, trust in killing
prevails. But our story is longer than this.

March of the Mothers

They came in waves to sweep across the square—
was that the crash of the sea?—no, they were
shouting names of sons, and yes, in the roar
you could make out *Vasily . . . Boris . . . Oleg*—
as they held against their breasts photos
of their boys stern in uniform with child eyes—
in the first wave photos of the dead, those mothers
wept and staggered, then raised each other up—
in the second wave photos of the wounded,
those mothers shrieked—then wave after wave,
faces who had not yet died, mothers muttering
*barracks are empty, graves are filling—do not
kill my son*—and high above along the parapet
the pigeons puffed their chests, colors flashing
in the sun—but no, it was a row of generals
dazzling their medals before they all fled,
for in the last wave came mothers of the generals
commanding them down from their perch with
Shame . . . Shame . . . Shame.

Accessory to War

Last glimpse before
dark: crushed mint in a bowl
for tea, pewter pot with the bent spout,
and my brother sprawled on the carpet singing
me to sleep, the song our grandmother sang to our
mother under the olive trees in the mist of her stories
that were our book of delights, night by night
the telling of the time before, gardens
and bread, water from the well,
doves in the fig tree, then
starlight on the roof.

Reading the news, I learn
my taxes bought one rivet on the shoulder
of a bomb that fell on a family, my rivet flung
free as shrapnel whistling through the room to blind
a child so her brother clawing through smoke and rubble
vowed revenge in all directions, his life for retaliation—war
works so well for enemies, making each other seem
necessary, while my taxes, dirty money earned
by teaching and writing, bought the rivet
on the shoulder of the bomb
this poem sent.

Thinking about Poets in Myanmar
while Pulling Thistles

You may have tough gloves, an iron fist
to blunt the thorns that prick your wrist,
tickle your mind. We have deep roots.

Your only tool is a blade to pry one root,
then another from stones and earth.
We are millions, millions.

Count on your fingers the roots you have
dug up. Burn them. Study your heap of ash.
Tell yourself that's it.

But miss one, we'll send seeds, millions
to settle on your shoulders, in your hair,
in mud on your boots. And look—

everywhere—new thistles underfoot.

Child in the Corn Field

Once, sorting mail, out of the blue came a poem
from a man who takes his sleepless newborn son
for a drive in the wee hours, and when his baby sleeps,
he writes little human stories under a streetlight
where all is quiet.

So I wrote him back, and we discussed poetry
and infancy and virtues of the very early morning
until for what he perceived as my kindness, he wrote me
about his sister, who had been a soldier
in Afghanistan.

And so I wrote to her about the importance of her
brother's poetry, and she sent me a small collection
of her own—poems about what goes on even
as war goes on: the chance life
of children.

And from inside her book fell a postcard of a child
in a corn field, somewhere high above the fighting
and I cried, looking out at the haze of trouble
beyond this moment of golden stillness
where our future stood alone.

First Responder at a Time of Grief

When hurt hits someone near you
and they sprawl, knocked flat by impact,
their scene of trouble bright with shattered
certainties, and others are wounded, still
and solo, as all around you people dither,
a ring of ashen faces, hollow eyes, all stunned
to silence by catastrophe, no one stepping close
to act, for that's impossible, and you first feel
helpless and afraid—you may be the one to do
what must be done to move the story forward
with first words, to keep time moving with a touch,
to drench your hands with the blood of grief,
give your coat to the coldest, save the life
still able, bind the injury, treat for shock.
Be not afraid to do it wrong—you've been
training for this all your life.

Plum Trees in War

How do they do it?—no resistance,
no complicity, simply opening
a new species of light bud by bud
in spite of all we have burned and broken.

As enemies prepare their advance
across hills and fields, spring
got there first, took possession
and raised its million flags of green.

From the sky, breath by breath,
the command comes down, so every
soldier says, "I can't kill today—
I am busy blossoming."

3.

Manhood Lost and Found

Her Name Was Scholastica
   but She Went by Schully

In green taffeta, our teacher stood petite on her
toes in a trance, eyes blazing, spittle trembling
at her lips reciting Whitman's spells and psalms,
Emily's enigmas, hewn meditations of Thoreau as
she gazed long and steady, each of us caught in her
searchlight of love. Then she whispered, "Take out
your journal, and write of fire in your soul that both
hurts and feeds you honey." Thus, she buried me
in rapture, alone with my flames, scribbling in
fury my thorns, my wilderness of fear and desire.

Now, fifty years beyond her whispered sermons
to my heart, that tattered notebook wears a halo,
an aura no one else can see, my secrets scrawled,
heaped, spilled forth ragged in code. And in
the margin, as a bird might write with a tiny
red pen, her words: *Some would divide life
into youth and adulthood. Do not divide
yourself! You will still be who you are
fifty years hence. Don't ever let
yourself be lost.*

Back Then, His Words
Were Not Enough . . . Now
They Are Precious

We stopped on a road in Montana.
My father sat on the passenger side.
I turned off the car and poured out
my sorrows, my life falling apart,
all my landmarks gone.

He was silent. We listened to the river.
Two crows flew over. They could go
anywhere. The river flowed silver.
My father put his hand on my sleeve:
"Be of good heart, my friend."

On a Hill in Scotland
My Brother and I Decide to Be Bad

Set loose when he was yet alive
on that long green steep, smooth as lawn,
we found these boulders, half-sunk stone
cannonballs you could pry free to send
hurtling down, spinning, bouncing,
bounding to sail, aimed for the road
but hey, no cars, so we did one after another,
gleeful, giddy dancing in transgression, all of
thirteen and twelve in our sudden pleasure to be free
from moderation, wind slapping our grinning mugs, sweat
flung from our faces as we worked and laughed like never,
ever, until—until he straightened, held up one
hand, bent down, reached deep
into his divot, pulled up a book
buried there, green, ragged, ancient,
secret, sacred, precious, and with
trembling hands, he . . . —but in a gust
pages exploded into tatters flickering,
fluttering, fleeing blasted wild and gone
to the sky—as years later he did—
unread, secret, sacred, precious.

Bobo

That's what we called her because
she was slow. In our junior high
she never could be Barbara—she
had this goofy smile, and stumbled.
In the hall one day—chaos in a river
of bodies fevered with change—she
smiled at me, hopeful. She liked me
so I stuck out my tongue at her.
She cried. She sobbed, her body
crumpled inward, a standing heap.
I was called to the principal. My
defense? "I was sticking out my tongue
at someone else, behind her."
As if my lie made that okay.

Barbara, I know you never can
forgive me. I call you by your name.

My Greatest Compliment Ever

It was the sixties, in Barcelona's train station,
I was a scruffy vagabond talking with an old lady,
babbling my instinctive high school Spanish as I
lifted her bag into a cart, and she asked me to find
her son, a tall man, she said, with a felt hat, who
would be smoking a cigarette, distracted, checking
his watch, and we laughed over travelers' frenzy
swirling all around us . . . and then she said, "*¿Señor—
es usted extranjero?*" (Sir, are you a foreigner?)

Oh, she knew who I was—American kid AWOL
from home with rucksack and sturdy boots—but she
chose to smile for the sweetest of moments, with a kindness
I have savored these fifty years, as if she had taken me
for her countryman, *un joven de su país.*

Deschutes, 1979

A hard time, age 29, gone wrong
from this life, lost from any sense
of strength, astray from happiness,
aimless, driving east I came

to a desert river shining
under a big moon, left my car,
shed my clothes, stepped sharp
stony ground to ease in

until its current had me, cradle
holy where my left hand held
a midstream boulder, let my
body be ribbon loose

to sway and flicker, helpless,
lost from lonely into
all those waters offered
from some endless source.

Footnotes to the Unspeakable

Once in the early '60s[1]
on a spring morning my brother[2] and I
were scrambling[3] through a ravine
below the baseball field, when a ball[4]
came out of the sky and hit
my brother[5] on the head, and he cried
and I cried[6] with him, and above the bank
appeared the face of an older boy[7]
who said over his shoulder
to his buddies, "Looks like
we hit two birds[8] with one stone."

—Kim Stafford[9]

1. This was before JFK was killed, then Martin, then Bobby.
2. Death by suicide, 7 November 1988: pistol to the head.
3. We avoided the straight path, liked to hide.
4. The crack of a bat sounded like a pistol shot.
5. He was older than me, but shorter, and this bothered him.
6. We were one body.
7. A boy who later died in Vietnam.
8. A bird in a thicket singing is my brother now.
9. Author of *100 Tricks Every Boy Can Do: How My Brother Disappeared*.

When Silence Is Loud

Late fall, by the lake at dusk,
when all boats have gone
and the wind dies down, we
push our listening into stone
silence, all sound gone home
to sleep, trees holding breath,
water chilled to stillness,
leaving us numb.
                    So we
will be when one among us
goes, when one story stops,
one voice becomes that lake
at dusk—beautiful, reticent,
hinting with light across
the water what no one
needs to say.

Lost in Snow

When all day falling the white sky fills
every track back to the road for home, when
turning you see every tree is every tree by
camouflage in their blank circumference,
when no matter how you pivot you can't find
a path, when recognition dawns at dusk you are
lost for the night, there is nothing for it now—
it's then you choose a hemlock or a fir,
a trunk with no low limb to impede your need,
and with your left glove on the dim bark begin
to circle your certain spindle, counting your
stamped circuits of a hundred, two, then three,
or counting breaths that puff more precious as cold
deepens and the dark drifts close, knowing if you
wander you are doomed, if you sleep you are gone,
but tramping endless circles will convey you
safe to sunrise.
                              So by grief
you say his name softly to yourself as you orbit
the vacant place he was to be dizzy with it, you say
his syllable through dark days, through changing
moons around and around in place, but not deeper
into the dark wood where no one could find you.
Oh my tree, plain companion, root and anchor.

Furry Dice

for Doug

From the rearview mirror of your muscle car,
black fuzz & white dots swivel at every skid
to show who's got *cojones*, whose death
wish gamble peals to skid, all four wheels
smoking at cliff curves when inches
from the brink you grab a gear.

One way to live is to *live*, brother—
push balance, crowd the odds,
shoulder through thickets of restraint
until you stand at knife edge, bold
with bright eyes staring down
terror with a grin.

Or check this out: furry dice flailing
from the boom of our Hobie Cat ripping top
speed tipped on one fin screaming over waves
just before we flipped at peak thrill, flung
deep into the drink. Those were the days, brother—
double six, pair of threes, snake eyes!

The Knot of Your Enigma
Unravels Me

You are a contradiction, a problem I love
to solve, but never solve. You are a blessing
so neatly disguised as a paradox, I spend my
waking in a puzzle, and my dreams in awe.

A thirsty abundance, you wake to tell me
you have nothing, blind to your beauties
concentric as a Russian doll, a bud opening
petal by petal before my eyes.

You came to me from nowhere, appearing
from everywhere like a birdcall or the sky,
until I knew you as my oxygen
sent by a forest far away.

Looking at you, I see mirrored rain,
reflection spangle, prism of affection,
mountain spring of songs where I bow
to sip your lips.

If Not for You

If not for the moon, we would be poor—
no silver to rim the leaves, the night
garden dark with starlight.

If not for feathers, not a single song
from thickets pleading our allegiance
to the winsome unseen.

If not for rain, the sea would starve
saltless, never tasting mineral clues
to mountain secrets.

If not for you, the moon would preside
over this empty house where birds
sing eulogy for what might have been . . .

if not for you.

Gone to the Garden

In Viet Nam, when one retires,
people say, *về vườn* . . . Our friend
has "gone to the garden."

Now my garden appoints the seasons.
Now I take calls from jay and crow
as I open a row in dark earth.

Now I confer with seed of beet and gourd,
and with a tent of sticks and string
I offer the bean vines a path to heaven.

Instead of paper, mulch.
Instead of clock, dawn and dusk.
Instead of memo, memory—

bowing over potato ground
I greet my father's shadow
lifting the hoe.

Lowbrow Epiphany

Me, I'm an old coot trying to get by with
coffee early, beer late, and between I look
at the sky, look in people's eyes, I study
shadows under trees to see if I can find
revelations of the obvious, how things
dawn on me slowly, sort of sneak up on me,
dropping hints the size of Cadillacs till
I get it, till I'm a raccoon fiddling with
a wad in muddy water where I unwrap
the ugly to find the lovely, or maybe I'm
a mechanic tuning a busted car until
it makes that sweet song starting,
running, racing, or maybe I'm an old
dog with one trick left but that's enough
to call death's bluff, and honor everyone.

Two Bums with Beer

I was nineteen—no map, just rucksack,
sleeping bag and wood flute hitching
north, and hungry. In a shop I bought
bread and cheese, two bottles, slunk
up a hill, found a space inside the thicket,
arrayed my precious delights—then he
stepped ragged from shadows
to grin at my bottles, then at me.
Opening both, I held one out, we
clinked our bitter bubbles, and drank.

How much have I hoarded since,
hard miser of joys, as if I would be less
by sharing my bounty with a stranger
as I did that day in Sweden.

Old Codger's Garden of Verses

More like a weed patch, really—my low road
to Boghall, my insomnia tunnel of regrets, my path
through gorse and adders, my glimpse of greatness
through a screen of trees. But then that crazy sun
spindled through clouds to make luminous
what once was dark and strange:

I saw a black dog swimming the river.
The jackdaw's bickering gave me a shiver.
For the bells of my memory not yet rung
the tang of the blaeberry bit my tongue.
Up like a swing my mood is bright—
And my good luck grows when I revel right.

Rainy Day in the '40s

When my parents were in love and poor
just after the war, a hungry Sunday on Filbert Street
in San Francisco they trod the pavement feeling glum.

Where Telegraph Hill came down they heard a sound,
looked up to see no one but an apple gleaming red,
rolling down into my father's hand, and with his knife,

divided, it became their gritty sacrament they taught us:
bounty in small will be enough to fill your hand or cup
when hard times come.

Be kind, hold on, and remember to look up.

A Chair by the Creek

Someone spoke twisted words to hurt you,
control you, tarnish your name. Good thing
you have this chair out under the cottonwoods
where leaves swivel trouble away.

A nosy neighbor shouts across the property line—
something about your right to be. Good thing those
words were swallowed by the friendly rattle
and chuckle of the creek.

Settled in your chair, enchanted by moving water,
your thoughts turn green, your heart fills with
slanted sunlight, whisper of aspen. You put all
words of envy, anger, and greed into the sound

of moving water, and listen as they flow away.

Forest Ranger

"What do you want to be," they asked,
"when you grow up?" To me, it was simple:
I would wear green, live in a cabin by a lake,
and protect the forest . . . or maybe a lookout high
on a mountain scanning horizons for smoke.
My hands would smell of pitch, and I would tell
stories by a big campfire to shining eyes of children.
Even in high school, when I heard about Thoreau
I thought that guy had the right idea: live in a hut
and just walk around. "Saunter," I think he said.

In college, though, I got practical—English major—
and spent my career indoors with books and ideas.
But then, in age, I bought a green hat, and began
to range the forest, inspecting old trees, listening
to mountain streams and wild birds, sauntering
along trails with only a pen and notebook, then off
into wild hills, gazing into the distance from
any high place. My job has become the writing
of an environmental impact statement to save
the forest, song by song, story by story.

Rich Land Between

for Perrin

In a forest wilderness many years ago
you appeared to me, and I appeared to you—
two birds in separate trees singing to the sky.

We looked down to find the ground between us
illuminated by a story we wanted to live. I could
see it with your eyes, and you with mine.

Since then, we have explored the land between—
every crumb of earth, every stem golden by day,
withering by season, sprouting again and again

until it's hard to tell where your song ends
and mine begins. The land between, crisscrossed
by these devotions, has revealed how in our life

the gifts are many, and the price is everything.

Sweeping Dew from Sage

1.

Far from the car near Harney Lake, I stood with my father
to study a zigzag petroglyph tapered to a circle knob
held high. "Is it lightning?" I asked. He pointed behind me
where a rattlesnake slid slowly into a cleft. I pointed
behind him where another unraveled its coil to sidle
into shadow. By the prickle on the back of my neck,
I was learning to read.

2.

As she wove willow sticks peeled pale into the dream-shade
for a cradleboard, a desert grandmother told me how
when an infant sheds its umbilical knot, that nub is sewn
into a tiny pouch of smoke-tanned doeskin and tied
to a juniper limb in the hills. "Then that child, growing,"
she said, "will always feel home, pulling." In the silence
after her words, I was learning to listen.

3.

Far from the car I stood with my brother on a dirt track
leading through sage toward Glass Butte. Something had
stopped us, something in silence had spoken, and we turned,
oblique to study the horizon. The whole circumference
roved unencumbered by the human, and as I gazed around,
stillness was so deep I could hear sinews in my neck
crackle, as if we were already ghosts come back to learn
this way of belonging.

4.

I have been told in the time before, in the time before, in
the time before, in winter a desert band might gather turning
around a piñon pine by starlight, woven into one ring by arms
on each other's shoulders, and dance that circle round and round
all night singing a one-line song: *Toward the tree with pine nut
cone seeds in the mountains we move about. Toward the tree
with pine nut cone seeds in the mountains we move about.*
From that story I hungered to know my way to bless.

5.

Leaving the car, I walked out onto the bridge
over the Crooked River, the bridge where my brother
stood a long time, looking down, the morning before
he put a pistol to his head and left us. I walked
onto the bridge to look down, to try to see what he
had seen, that hard welcome of killing shadow
far below, luring him, promising rest from pain.
A breath came up from the canyon, cold and blue,
his pain right there. I must keep learning how to live.

6.

They say among some desert people, the Milky Way
offers the dusty trail to the other world a spirit follows
after life. They say it is danger to look directly at a whirlwind,
which might be a human spirit traveling. They say it is not polite
to point at a rainbow, nor wise to follow a butterfly. They say
it is wrong to gesture toward lightning, not safe for young boys
to be seen by too many stars, who are women, and might
bring them illness, desiring them as husbands. They say thunder

is a kind of badger who, when lifting his chin to the sky, and
bringing it down, makes rain come. So to learn, I look closely
at little things, and bring my chin down.

7.
Far from the car one night, sleeping near Fort Rock,
I woke over and over to bristling stars, a bird singing
tireless, thriving in the little Eden of its song, singing its
one line over and over as the desert people did,
dancing around the piñon pine. Small witness
in a big place: I was taught the sufficiency of the spare.

8.
They say among desert people a woman could be
shaman as well as a man. Her calling came through
a spontaneous dream. She was taught to forget
her power between times that gift was needed,
and to lead an ordinary life. Like other desert beings—
whirlwind, raven, butterfly, coyote—such a dreamer
would travel in obscurity, until something required
the transformation to shaman, then the resonance
would come. By this I learned how from the ordinary
you must rise into helpful dreaming—as dry trees
reach up eager into the storm, as the whirlwind rises,
as coyote wails to the hard stars.

9.
One time far from the car, southwest from Brothers,
as I followed a track old cars had made before they rusted
into scrap and joined a heap to be forgotten up a ravine

behind a ranch that failed, I came upon a post leaning
with two arrowed signs, one aimed south and inscribed
in faded script: *San Francisco*, and the other reaching north:
The Dalles. I looked south and north along that highway of dust,
where dull green sage ached to close the seam.

10.
Some desert people would say
Don't chase your soul, meaning Don't go too fast.
Or they would say, *I will pay you when I die*, meaning
At my funeral you will receive gifts. Or sometimes,
to warn against outside tricksters, they would say,
*When Coyote arrives at a place, he speaks the people's
language well*. Or, *When walking in the brush, don't speak
the name of rattlesnake*. Instead say, *Little Waving One*.
And *If you don't dance, the bear will bite you*.
You say such things where only the stones listen,
but they listen with great patience and skill.

11.
South from Lakeview, a badger faced me
from a burrow, gray eyes dim with dreaming, not needing
to be fierce, so utterly in command. We stared, I the upright
child, and he the old shaman shouldering earth, lifting his chin,
then bringing it down as he backed into darkness,
shoveling earth behind him to close the burrow door.
I stood alone, as sudden rain began.

12.
They say some foraging bands would range
over the land, radiating from a known landmark-hub
toward a shifting periphery. No boundaries, only a center—
a spring, a mountain, a place for ritual—under the Pleiades
(*Coyote's Daughters*), under the moon (*Your Father's Father*).
They brushed dew from sage tips with the wing of a duck
into a willow bottle sealed with pitch, then ran to feed the children
bundled in rabbit-skin blankets in a shelter of brush open to the south.

13.
One time driving the Ochocos with my brother,
a two-lane dusty track descending the mountain,
a swale, a cabin sagging forgotten, we pried open the door:
tattered curtains, kerosene lamp dry on the table,
shreds of purple velvet peeling from walls. "How
would it be," my brother said, "to live here always?"

14.
They say when the people hunted, they hunted for spirit,
a matter of focus, of concentration on exact details
that include whole stories—a piñon pine that gives
everything, a circling hawk that sees everything, a river
in dry country that gathers all creatures into one living web,
rose hips beaded red and threaded on a stem of grass
around a child's neck for beauty at the dance.

15.
North from Grandview, far from the road,
I sat all afternoon in the shade of an ancient juniper,
remembering the many-legged petroglyph old ones pecked
on that boulder near where the Crooked River slid into the Deschutes
before the dam buried that known center in deep darkness
and the sacred had to live in stories. Reaching arms around me,
the juniper was teaching me, with twisted limbs, contortions
I would suffer, reaching this way and that to obey the sun—
father gone, brother gone, night bird singing, badger
bringing rain, whirlwind walking a spirit home, and all of us,
all of us dancing around the pine tree chanting
desert words of blessing.

4.

Your Emily Dickinson Hour

Poetry-Monger

Why condemn these thrills to the smithy
where iron-mongers thrust rusted rods in fire
then pound them white-hot thin to bend, curl,
and writhe unto their will? I love sparks to fly
when I burn words so they surrender their integrity
and fuse—twisted, welded, sealed. Desk my anvil,
pen my punch, word-hoard my ware I feed through
the thought-forge to be reduced to syllables hammered
into arabesque, swirl and grid, wrapped and riveted,
quenched with a hiss billowing steam, then lifted
dripping, gleaming, new-born from dark dreams.
Is it any wonder my hands are scorched and scarred,
my gaze seared, my lungs filled with fire?

Book Store

From the street, steps lead down to paradise.
At the door, a bell rings when readers enter.
Tall walls form canyons of secret stories.
A ladder on wheels stands ready for climbing.
On the shelves, between books, typewriters
each hold a page with a paragraph or stanza
from a book nearby. On the wall, framed,
a letter from a writer proclaims love for the store.
Behind the counter, the owner, reading a book,
looks up in welcome. In the back corner, under
a window lit green by trees, intent at a tiny desk,
a child is writing, her pencil scratching the silence.

Poems for a Cause

What's your cause? What's your calling?
If it's justice, then pen a few just words
into a chant or song that can call us all
upright to witness and to testify.

If you believe education is key,
then compose a winsome proclamation
for a child to recite, standing small
but tall in the halls of power.

If it's Earth that tugs your heart,
or immigrant children who haunt
your dreams, or people by bad luck
cast out to camp under the overpass,

then find a way to sing these sorrows
into remedy, your hurt into help, syllables
to gather others, so words may guide our work,
and your pain be our refrain for change.

Words of Sugar, Words of Salt

Don't these times call for cayenne—
a taste to seize the mind in thrall?
What recipe can bring rogue judges
to their senses, bolster timid politicians,
feed the fat cats truth enough to cut
their purr? See that smoke curling
from the cook-off—forests on fire,
floods full, heat waves roasting us alive?
Maybe we're past hints and whispers,
our chance gone for subtle scents
and fugitive flavors—time for coffee
black, jolt of garlic, onion unadorned.

Your Finite Vote,
Your Infinite Voice

To vote, you blacken a box on paper,
you keystroke a blip on a screen,
you punch a hole in a ballot
and your hope becomes a number

for tabulation in democracy's machine,
one among millions, a seed of wheat
heaped in the granary, a drop of rain
seeking to quell the fires of confusion.

But you also have a voice—to speak,
to question, to imagine, to sing, to declare,
propose, honor, reveal, investigate, affirm,
console, discover, befriend.

How big is a vote?—one bead on a strand
of millions, one thorn scratch in mud, one
dimple left in sand by the centipede's
hind foot on its journey from dusk to dawn.

How big is a voice?—partaking of the sky,
inhaling wind and sending forth a song
that fills a room, and could turn the minds of many,
could build a vision for our great adventure.

While you count the river with a teaspoon, your
essential vote, you must also sing across the waters,
offering who you are to the long weaving work
of who we are for the days to come: in many, one.

To Lend a Hand

I was discord and my teacher tuned me.
I was an empty cup and a stranger filled me.
I was a dry seed when my mother put me
in earth, fed me rain. I was the stray dog
my friend took in, gave bowl and bed.

Discord, cup, and seed—a helper seeks
a stranger's need. I was the silence
you sang. I was the bell you rang. You
baked the bread, left each secret said,
took my hand for where our journey led.

What's Not in the News

People use their eyes not to see
beauty, but to avoid danger.
—Joel Meyerowitz

Sunrise doesn't make front page.
What stringer quotes my mother's ghost?
Who shall report a child's opinion?
A vagabond's obituary? An inmate's
joke in the funny pages?

Instead, the roving eye of the news
swivels toward trouble, tragedy,
the work of big money and mean souls:
tell the tough, but hide the tender . . .
spotlight death, leave birth in shadow.

And of what of peace, joy, devotion?
That's up to every voice among us.

Schooling Sorrow

When a sorrow's young, it's pure—stunned
pang at breakup, betrayal, failure, death.
You weep, rant, brood, slump. And then

in the morning, sorrow starts its epic
journey into memory, becomes an island
in your archipelago of sufferings.

Then, if you are strong, and lucky to have
a listener—you begin to apprehend its quirks,
to tell it, shape it, watch it grow into a story.

And if you tell your story well, with curiosity
and courage, it then becomes a possession,
and in time a treasure, a smudge of wisdom.

This can be your gift, your offering—but
if you don't school your sorrow into story
it can never be your friend.

Voice Mail

You have reached the number of a person
too busy to answer, and the mailbox is full.
Sorry to say, sending a fax would be futile.
You could try again tomorrow and tomorrow
and tomorrow. Are you getting the message?
If so, press 1, and you may hang up and
be blessed. If not, please press 2, and you
may wait on the line as long as you like.

While you are waiting, remember: the means
of communication are constantly improved,
while our substance of communication remains
in a dark age. Are you ready to ask the burning
question, to say what must be said? If so, write
a letter to get your words right—or a poem, story,
manifesto to make your meaning clear, to open
your heart, to make plain your love's hard truth.

Connoisseur of the Blank Page

What do I know of completion,
publication, fame—of the book deal,
magisterial review, top of the chart?

Any proof of brilliance in finished work—
isn't that a little boring, being done,
boxed in a book, inert?

I prefer the hesitant pen poised
over the blank page, hungry for hint,
twinge, prickle of apprehension.

Isn't this our life now, a predicament
of profound uncertainty, old answers
failed, unknown acts our one hope?

So I prefer a scribble's thrill across
the empty, stepping along dusky with
ignorance, clumsy through silence,

lurching, groping, turning the head
for that thread of song epiphany sings
somewhere just ahead.

Den of Words

Because it's dark, I do my work
by feel. Before my heap of shaggy
thoughts, I kneel to gnaw cold bones
of old hurt, then badger trouble into song.
I scrawl my visions on these walls—
all I can bear of anguish and fear: horse,
bull, and running deer. I turn earth scent
of moss, burnt stone, and some stink of fox
into story after story, chanting river's thrum
and storm's glory with my salty tongue. Stars
wheel, night dawns, winter turns as I worry
our syllables of pain into healing charms
for kits and cubs. Seeking essence, I sling
my lingo of sensation, singing dreams of leaf,
fin, wing, and hand. And when my work
is over, will you lead me blinking to the sun?

Contemplation

The word has *temple* in it, and
elation. Something *placid*, *peaceful*,
syllables asking for a settled time,
even if only a moment, a breath.

It's right there, always, inside the burly
administration of a life, the rush
and tumble haste—a room in time,
an altar, a space to bow and listen.

Frenzy has a heart and it is this:
cast off ambition's harness,
set down your tools of doing,
dwell here in silence. Be the bell.

Your Emily Dickinson Hour

You can't have it all day? Who says
you can't have it for an hour—
a pocket of attentive freedom
while others sleep, or stare

at screens, shackle to phones,
capitulate to life's administration.
You must scribble feverish
some feral apprehension

on an envelope's back,
ghost haunting the house,
the belle of your own life,
recluse under a tree where

shadow fretted majesty—
the shutters—of the sun
gash your breathless agony
before—the fire is gone.

Why No Longer a Wild Bird

When I fell out of the music at about
age two, they said, *Here's a bowl and spoon,*
but with my wings I found them hard to hold.

Then they said, *Here are words—you can
use them instead*, but I found it hard to fit
my singing into syllables.

They said, *Now you don't need to fly.*
They put me in a car, and soon
my thicket was far behind.

Still, sometimes before day, the dark aches
and my heart grows great in silence
as the sky begins to change.

Canary in the Mind

If you descend to sorrow, take a little singer
to carry through the dark some color of the sun.

Tunneling through trouble, guard your little light,
shield your little singer for the good of everyone.

If your singer falters, if your mind goes dim,
if your breath grows shallow, if your days grow grim,

feed your little singer seeds of hope again.
In the cave of grief, with every breath begin.

Afterword: As Poetry Begins to Change

Many of the poems in this book came to the page in the old way: something occurred to me "out of nowhere," and as I started to write, that first thought grew into something else—the customary miracle of creation. I remembered a time in the desert . . . I heard birds singing in the dark before dawn . . . I thought about Emily Dickinson . . . and I wrote in response to these inklings. I remembered my high school English teacher, and had to write "Her Name Was Scholastica." I felt grief at the death of a friend, and had to write "Lost in Snow" to companion his partner. I sat in silent online meditation with Buddhists in Ukraine, and had to write "Mother Russia, Wounded by the Modern Tsar" and other poems in solidarity. But the way these poems gathered for this book grew from a shift I sense in how poems now work in the world. For the book includes a number of the short poems I have posted on Instagram the day I wrote them, and my venture into this custom has a story.

Once at a big literary conference I went, as a skeptic, to a session called "Poetry & Instagram." Going in, I was curious, though I considered my poems "too important" to be littered online. Confirming my disdain, an expert explained to us that Instagram could be a platform for experimental forays with language, and a great place to market your published work, but dedicated writers should never post new poems online, he said, because such a poem is thus technically "published," and can no longer be submitted to a literary magazine. Instagram for marketing, he said, and magazines for literature.

As I listened, though, I realized a new poem posted on the Web could be read—right now—by hundreds, or thousands of people, instead of only by those who seek their literature in print, often in magazines largely read by poets. And it often took me months, or years, to place a poem in such a magazine. What if someone in grief or confusion or loneliness needed a poem right away, a poem I might be hoarding? What if I wanted to share a poem with people in real time—today, this moment—perhaps for people who don't read journals or books? Why not harness my daily writing practice, and reach out by posting in all directions?

When I discussed this with my daughter, who has used social media for years to share work as a "floral innovator," she pressed me to post my poems online with abandon. Her own images blossom on various sites, and she convinced me to lean into this practice. She pointed out that poems come to me in abundance, so why hold back on letting them flow forth toward readers? There would always be more where those came from, she said. The source is infinite, and the need is now.

I began to see that readers and writers are both, in the end, anonymous in the wide world, and the moment of reading is where they grope from different directions to make something together—an understanding, an insight, a challenge or consolation. During moments of reading, poems take shape in the air between writer and reader, while they are simultaneously engaged in what is happening in the world now. To wait for eventual publication in a magazine could be like two friends saying to each other "Hey, we should get together—sometime . . . " instead of "Are you busy right now? Let's sit down and talk."

I already had a daily writing practice that generally resulted in a poem of some sort each morning. So I started posting occasional poems on Instagram, and in the process learned several things. First, such a poem will be short, roughly square, to fit the online Instagram grid. Second, I began to feel I was not writing poems, exactly, but addressing readers with texts shaped like poems, as I sought to accompany these readers in the moments of trouble and confusion the world dishes out daily. Third, by writing and posting, I could respond directly to the day's news, often addressing events in a way outside journalism—for the news is crowded with prompts-in-the-moment. I could follow the poem with a companion photograph to highlight an image in the poem, emphasize an idea in the poem, or talk back to the poem by showing something oblique. And finally, as I posted daily, there would sometimes be comments on the poems by readers out there—gratitude, rebuttal, question, a furthering thought.

About the time I started writing many of the poems in this book, in 2018, I was beginning my term as Oregon's Poet Laureate, a public ambassador for poetry. As I presented over a hundred in-person events in communities across the state, my task was to be the friendly diplomat, inviting all kinds of people into the experience of evocative language in a spell of words, into ways a poem can offer both writers and readers a swift, deep leap into memory, prophecy, challenge, and peace.

Then in 2020 when the pandemic hit and lockdown came, I had to cancel my remaining twenty-five events as Poet Laureate, my face-to-face encounters in classrooms, libraries, and community centers. To keep serving as public poet, I decided to use my daily writing practice to compose and post a new poem every morning on Instagram and Facebook as a way to share solace, thought, challenge, humor, and companionship through our hard time. I was writing poems for "the common reader," and this shaped how I wrote, striving, as Sir Philip Sidney advised in the sixteenth century, to think like a philosopher, but speak like a common person—rather than the other way around. Often, my daily prompts were the news, but I found the news incomplete. The news told what had happened, what was said—or tweeted—but not what this meant, what this called us to ask, to ponder, to do. So in each day's poem, I tried to write about something behind the news, or in spite of the news—to speak in the voice of a nurse in despair . . . in the voice of a confused president . . . in the voice of Shakespeare recognizing the quirky character of our time . . . in the voice of a soldier on the battlefield calling home. I felt I was not so much a writer composing original poems, as I was a courier delivering, directly from events to readers, little anthems of thought.

My initial goal was to post daily as long as the pandemic lasted, but as that danger began to wane, there were plenty of other mysteries and terrors to address, and I've kept the daily custom since. For in this practice, I came to a new sense of my role as a writer. Though many poems weren't right for posting online, adding this outlet to my repertoire shaped my sense of vocation. As I said in one of my online posts, "When I make breakfast, do I make a breakfast for the ages? No. When I write, do I write for the ages? No. I write for today, for a reader now, for you." My impulse to let poems brim forth from the moment of their making now reaches beyond online poems to include self-published chapbooks I produce to give away, poems etched in stainless steel at public locations, a poem in calligraphy on the wall in our local children's hospital, poetry postcards I print to send in all directions, and other forms of gift economy for the poetic task.

This all makes me wonder how the experience of writing and reading poetry has changed for you. Do you sense that poetry has slipped out the side door from the palace of literature to become a liberated instrument to empower change in your daily life? There will always be another election of some sort on the horizon, where beyond your finite vote the world needs your infinite voice.

As I was assembling this book, I wrote to my friend Alireza Taghdarreh in Tehran, a scholar of Rumi and translator of Thoreau and Emerson into Farsi, and asked him what many people had asked me: "What can poetry do, really, for our world on fire?" Ali wrote back that this was the wrong question. People should be asking, he said, "What can violence do? What can wars do? What can money do, finally, to really help us? Poetry is oxygen. Poetry makes it possible to live."

In recent years we have known erratic politics, the pandemic, the "Me Too" movement, protests following the death of George Floyd, fires in forests around the world, a contested election, violence in our Capitol and in our schools, and our sustained and catastrophic war on the Earth itself, where we burn the sky. And by the time this book comes out, I suspect there will be no shortage of traumas and enigmas in the human project that might be addressed by poems helping readers live.

In the face of our daily onslaught, I've sensed readers reaching for poetry to seek perspective, sustain their spirits, not feel so alone, and form resolve for remedy. As the writer Gary Miranda has said, "People who do not write or read poetry are spared the inconvenience of thought." But thought is now a saving commodity, in individual lives, and in our national and global destiny. I believe that for many, poetry may once have been a luxury—but now could save our lives by nudging us all toward waking our collective powers. So this book ends with a series of poems that have grown from my calling as a teacher, my habit of inviting others into the practice of writing, a hands-on search for peace in ourselves for the world. Here's what I might say to my class in a last session, as I sent them forth to relish delving into the experience of writing:

Dialect Spoken by One

From the common tongue, you utter
a lingo unique from all—how could it
be otherwise? For sunset burns your heart,
no mercy, and moonlight ladles into you
a kind of strange, and dreams finger your soul,
fumbling to whittle who you are, last of a lost
people, solo exile, vagabond muttering a wisdom
that can only be chanted by your way of saying,
even if only understood by the ancestors crowding
in spirit at your back. So speak to them now over
your shoulder, and speak for them to the living
what will be lost forever if you don't hold forth
unafraid, like a bird singing before dawn.

Biographical Note

Kim Stafford is a writer and teacher in Oregon, and founding director of the Northwest Writing Institute at Lewis & Clark College. His poetry titles include *A Gypsy's History of the World* (Copper Canyon Press) and *Singer Come from Afar* (Red Hen Press). He has published a biography, *Early Morning: Remembering My Father, William Stafford* (Graywolf Press); a memoir, *100 Tricks Every Boy Can Do: How My Brother Disappeared* (Trinity University Press); a book about writing and teaching, *The Muses Among Us: Eloquent Listening and Other Pleasures of the Writer's Craft* (Georgia University Press); and a children's book, *We Got Here Together* (Harcourt Brace). With Charles Finn he has edited *The Art of Revising Poetry: 21 U.S. Poets on Their Drafts, Craft, and Process* (Bloomsbury Press). Poems in this book have appeared in literary journals and anthologies, and been chosen for the Academy of American Poets Poem-a-Day series. His works have received Pacific Northwest Book Awards, and a Citation for Excellence from the Western States Book Awards. Stafford received two NEA Creative Writing Fellowships in poetry, and he has taught writing in Scotland, Italy, Mexico, and Bhutan. He cofounded the annual Fishtrap Writers Gathering in Oregon, and was chosen by Oregon governor Kate Brown in 2018 to be Oregon's Poet Laureate for a two-year term.

Printed in the USA
CPSIA information can be obtained
at www.ICGtesting.com
JSHW080442110224
57024JS00001B/2

9 781636 281476